Everything They Didn't Teach You in Seminary

†

Larry D. Holmes, Pastor

Jarretts Publishing House

Cover Photo by Joel Woodbridge

Faith is for the Living is available in print, and as a Kindle e-book through Amazon. Pastor's other ebooks, *Who is King?, I Can Because I'm Blessed,* and *Life's Delicatessen,* are available through most every ebook publisher including Kindle and Nook.

ISBN:

Printed in the U.S.A.

Dedication

To those men and women who, with trembling voice and firm handshake have said yes to God's call to serve in vocational ministry.

My humble desire is that you will find in these pages some insight and encouragement to the challenging task of ministry.

I am not sure where I read it; I just know the following is not mine originally. It does sum up my heart, however.

A prince came to his father and said he felt God was calling him into full time vocational ministry. Alas he would have to forgo his rightful place to the throne. The king responded to his firstborn with these words, "Son, if God has called you to be a minister, don't stoop to be a king."

Welcome to the royal work of kingdom building for the Master.

Table of Contents

Foreword

For nearly 20 years now, I have met with a wise sage to help guide me down this path some call ministry. This leader has taken me under his wing and has infused into me his wisdom and his grace. I am confident that he has influenced my life and ministry for the good. He has spoken wisdom into my life in moments when my lack of it was sadly, overwhelmingly, noticeable and I desperately needed to hear what direction, or some new idea, that would keep me going in the right direction. These were moments when my ministry had been strongly tested by decisions made by others that were not focused on Jesus.

In those moments, when I was confused and dejected, he lifted my head and gave me words that encouraged me to keep pushing through. I will forever be grateful for those times he took me out to eat, forced to have a meal when I was too dejected to have an appetite, yet he fed me more than food. He gave me exactly what I needed at that exact moment. Always.

This book is a journey with him down through the years of experience. To both read and implement these valuable bits of information would be a wise investment by anyone who is looking to be a better leader.

To have stayed in this church this long and to have fought through the storms he has had to face, only will the look on the Master's face be reward enough. He has fought through division, dissension, low dividends, death and dire circumstances to stand where he is today. Yes, he stands. He stands among leaders who made shortcuts, who gave up, who quit, who were not faithful, who were confused, who chose wrong paths and who willfully made bad choices. A man who has loved the ministry and has dedicated his life for one cause: that others may know Jesus.

As you read this practical guide, you, too, will find help in it. He will pour into you his many years of experience and, instead of you having to pay a high price through ignorance or bad decision-making, you will go forward with confidence after reading, and practicing, all that is between these covers. The price you pay for the book becomes priceless when you take and apply what he has shared.

I am confident, that what you are about to learn will help you as you sit across the table of this literary cafe and listen to this wise sage share life and ministry.

Prepare yourself for the journey. It will be well worth your investment of time and attention.

Phillip A Rhodes
District Superintendent
Joplin District, Church of the Nazarene

Introduction

When I accepted my first staff position as a female associate pastor, I had no idea what was involved in the daily routine of running a church. I had spent the last ten years as an evangelist, traveling with my husband and my family, singing and preaching. We would go to a church for the weekend and, after our last service, we would pack up and start the, sometimes, long journey back home or to another church. We didn't have to worry about the workings of the church, the budgets, staff meetings, getting volunteers, getting teachers for Sunday school or any other daily or weekly responsibilities within the church.

It wasn't until I was a part of a church staff that I really understood just what all went into being a pastor of a church congregation. I had read and studied the workings of the church and had studied the denominational guidelines, but I had never had any hands-on training until I became an associate pastor. Being a female pastor was not as well accepted then as it is in today's culture. After I was ordained, I was fortunate enough to be invited to go on staff at Wanamaker Woods. Here I have learned how to be a leader, how to conduct board meetings, how to do funerals, weddings, baptisms, serve communion and everything else that comes with being a pastor.

Even though I am a female pastor I am treated equally as a fellow pastor. Thanks to Dr. L D Holmes, and his leadership and teachings for his staff, I believe that I would be fully equipped to pastor a church if I ever felt God calling me in that direction.

I believe too many times we send young pastors right out of seminary, and even older first-time senior pastors, into a church to pastor and we don't fully equip them to do the job put before them. Unless they are fortunate enough to serve on staff where the senior pastor is a great mentor and teacher, they are unaware of even where to start shepherding their own flock. Sometimes they are asked to take on a huge task of salvaging a congregation that an ill-equipped pastor left in their wake. If that new pastor isn't well-equipped to know what and how to do what needs to be done, the church so many times doesn't grow spiritually or numerically. Pastors become disenchanted or discouraged and end up walking away from their calling. Many times pastors look at taking a church as a vocational job and are greatly disappointed in the results of their efforts because they were never really called by God to shepherd the flock.

It has been said that it takes a village to raise a child. In the same sense it takes a spirit-filled team to rise up a church. I Timothy 4:12-15 tells us, *"Don't let anyone look down on you because you are young, but set an example for the believers in speech, in conduct, in love, in faith and in purity. Until I come, devote yourself to the public reading of Scripture, to preaching and to teaching. Do not neglect your gift, which was given you through prophecy when the body of elders laid their hands on you. Be diligent in these matters; give yourself wholly to them, so that everyone may see your progress. Watch your life and doctrine closely. Persevere in them, because if you do, you will save both yourself and your hearers."*

I believe this guide for pastors is a valuable tool that needs to be in every new, and even not so new, pastor's library. By following this guidebook, and the information that is given in detail, one can conduct board meeting, conduct weddings, funerals, learn to be good stewards of God's resources, have great staff meetings, and shepherd the flock. They will be able to present themselves to God as one approved, a workman who does not need to be ashamed and who correctly handles the word of truth.

Pastor Fran Ruecker
Associate Pastor
Wanamaker Woods Church of the Nazarene
Topeka, Kansas

Acknowledgements

Every writer needs an Esther, truth teller, cheerleader, coach, critic and friend. There is nothing in print under my name that does not have her image stamped into every word. Thank you, Esther for your encouragement and helpful editing.

Every writer needs a helpmate who is patient, intelligent and positive. My wife of fifty-five years is that person. Thank you, Jolene!

Every writer needs a Jeff, that unique person who can see things through a different prism. You are that man, my friend. Thank you!

Every writer needs a Fran, someone who will proof-read the same thing time after time and still smile. Add to that the myriad of changes that demand changes. Thank you, Fran, for your attention to detail!

Every writer needs creative people around them. Thank you, Joel and Traci, for your cover creation!

Every writer needs a group of people who believe the best about them. The staff and wonderful people of The Woods at Wanamaker are just that. For thirty-five years we have traveled together through good times, difficult times, and great spiritual development times. I am so much better because they consistently invested their time, energy and love into me!

1

The Starting Place

I was twenty-six years old and feeling pretty good about life. God had blessed me with a career I enjoyed. I was married to a wonderful woman who God had gifted me with, and we had just welcomed our firstborn daughter.

It was on an early morning commute to work that things began to change. Seemingly out of nowhere I had this overwhelming sensation that God was calling me into the ministry. I call it a sensation because that is the only term that seems to fit. At first, I chalked it up to my assignment as a Sunday school teacher in our local church. I felt God must be wanting me to go deeper in my preparation for the classes. I was willing to do just that and pushed it to the back of my mind.

The next Sunday I presented a well-prepared presentation to my sixth grade Sunday school class. To say they were impressed would be a huge overstatement. They did not even seem to recognize my added work of prayer and preparation. But that was okay; I was doing what I felt God had been calling me to do.

The next week, I was once again confronted with the

realization that God was dealing with me about something. I just could not get away from the quiet voice that came unbidden at various times. By now I had begun to make friends with the thought that perhaps God was calling me into some type of ministry.

After about a month of personal introspection and questioning God I decided it was time to speak to my pastor. He listened very closely as I recounted my feeling that maybe God was calling me into the ministry. After asking several questions he said, "If the feelings you have aren't an expression of God communicating with you, they will eventually disappear. If they *are* God nudging you, the feelings will grow stronger. It's that simple."

Well, those feelings did not fade but became an increasing part of my daily thoughts. Of course, I shared these feelings with my wife. She assured me that she would support whatever I felt God was calling me to do.

I have heard some ministers say they ran from God's call. I cannot say that. Although I had a myriad of questions, I never once thought about turning or running from God or His call. I felt blessed, honored and humbled.

We eventually quit our jobs, moved out of our home, and made our way to Colorado Springs where we heard there was a new Bible College that would accept older students. That was almost fifty years ago, and I have no regrets. It has been a life of adventure and discovery that surprises me even today. God has allowed me to experience things far beyond my wildest dreams or thoughts.

I share this small vignette of my personal experience to highlight an important aspect of ministry. Real shepherds are called not hired! It was that call that kept me in the ministry when I wanted to run. It was that call that drew me back into ministry when I did run. I have never been able to get away from it!

So, what does the call of God upon a life look like?

I am reminded of what an old time preacher once said to me when I asked him just that question: "If you can do anything else and have the peace of God in your life, do it." I think what he was saying is that the call of God leaves no option. It is either service to The King of Kings or nothing.

Let me share a personal story with you.

In my second pastorate I became involved in a building campaign not of my choosing. I was told that if I did not "make it happen" then it would never happen. Quite a responsibility for one so young. At the time, I was in my senior year of college. I was carrying a full load as well as pastoring the church full time. In eighteen months, we raised the money for the project, tore down the old building, cleaned what lumber we could salvage for the new building and did all the work "in house". Fortunately, we had several skilled personnel with the necessary gifts and experience to bring the building together.

At the conclusion of those eighteen months I was done! I did not want to preach, make another hospital call, teach another class, or even perform the sacraments. I began to rethink my future. Maybe I had answered the call, but it was time to move on. I always thought I would like to be in law enforcement, so I applied for the highway patrol academy and the police academy the same week. Six weeks later I received a letter for an interview from both agencies. I chose the police academy because it allowed me to be at home with my family throughout the week. After graduating from the police academy, I was sworn in as a law enforcement officer in the largest police department in the state. I loved it. The friendships I made were special in a way difficult to explain. There was also something about putting bad people behind bars that I found fulfilling. Eventually I was promoted and began to teach new recruits. I had never enjoyed a job so much in my life.

The problem started one day as I was driving to work. It was like the Spirit of God came in and sat beside me in my car, although I have never heard the audible voice of God, I do know what it sounds like. It was like He said, "It is time for you to get back to doing what I called you to do!" Again, I could not get away from His insistent voice. There was no censure or feelings of guilt, just an overwhelming sense that things were going to be changing.

Within a few months I began sending my resume out to church leaders. Within six months I sold my personal police equipment and resigned my commission. I was back to pastoring full time.

Allow me to pause the story for just a moment and insert this reality. Without a wife who was sold on God and believed in her husband, I could never have climbed some of these hills. She never backed up or away. In fact, she was, and continues to be, my biggest cheerleader. She is truly a gift of God!

I share this story with you to highlight the fact that you cannot run from God's call. If indeed He has called you, you will never be able to do anything else.

I look back on my years as a police officer with great affection. There is no way I can say that I loved everything I experienced or had to do as a law enforcement officer. There are still some memories that visit me in the dark of night. But I so appreciate God giving me the opportunity to participate in the law enforcement community. It changed me in so many ways and I will be forever grateful.

There are those who may well challenge the call of God upon an individual to vocational ministry.

It is somewhat like the man in the Bible who was born blind, and Jesus healed. When confronted with critics of Jesus' ministry and His ability to heal, the man's response was classic: "Whether He is a sinner, I do not know; one thing I do know, that, whereas I was blind, now I see." I must confess in a very real way that too is my testimony. Oh, not about physical blindness, but about spiritual sight. I know what I know about God's call on my life. Anyone's acceptance or belief beyond that does not affect the reality of it!

There are those who might be inclined to look at vocational ministry as a job, or career choice. Without the call of God in such a life choice, I believe it is eventually doomed to failure.

A fair question that arises around the topic of "a God called ministry" is what about those whom God is calling to be Sunday School teachers, small group leaders, or other workers of the kingdom? Are these any less viable for God to use in promoting His Kingdom? Absolutely not! They are indeed servants of The Most High and are not only viable but necessary. However, I do think there is a distinction between "lay ministry" and "pastoral ministry." Both are called of God, both are necessary for the promotion of The Kingdom, and both are instruments of God.

There is a story from the Old Testament that I think will help illustrate this point.

"Now David again gathered all the chosen men of Israel, thirty-thousand. And David arose and went with all the people who were with him to Baale-judah, to bring up from there the ark of God which is called by the Name, the very name of the Lord of hosts who is enthroned above the cherubim. And they placed the ark of God on a new cart that they might bring it from the house of Abinadab which was on the hill; and Uzzah and Ahio, the sons of Abinadab, were leading the new cart. So they brought it with the ark of God from the house of Abinadab, which was on the hill; and Ahio was walking ahead of the ark. Meanwhile, David and all the house of Israel were celebrating before the lord with all kinds of instruments made of fir wood, and with lyres, harps, tambourines, castanets and cymbals. But when they came to the threshing floor of Nacon, Uzzah reached out toward the ark of God and took hold of it, for the oxen nearly upset it. And the anger of the lord burned against Uzzah, and God struck him down there for his irreverence; and he died there by the ark of God." II Samuel 6:1-7.

Was Uzzah a bad person? No! Was he just trying to be

helpful? Perhaps! The point of the story is that Uzzah was not commissioned by God to touch the ark! Touching what he should have not touched cost him his life.

As Dr. Eugene Stowe states in his seminal work *The Ministry of Shepherding*: Real shepherds are called, not hired. Jesus points up this truth in the passage immediately following His identification as the Good Shepherd (John 10:11-15) When the real cost of shepherding becomes apparent, hirelings are more interested in saving their own skins than in saving the sheep. Because His shepherding was a divine vocation - literally "calling"- Christ was ready to lay down His very life for the salvation of the flock.

A good Christian may or may not be a good shepherd. It is true, as Luther stated that there is a priesthood of all believers. Elton Trueblood correctly speaks of the ministry of the laity. However, scriptural evidence is conclusive that the Christian ministry must have its genesis in a definite divine call.

(The Ministry of Shepherding, pages 15-16)

Anything less than this certain sense of calling is inadequate preparation for successful shepherding.

In his book *Heralds of God* James S Stewart states: "… the ministry should not be regarded as a profession, a career, whose main qualifications are a certain amount of organizing ability, tact, and culture, the reputation of being a good 'mixer' and a shrewd judge of men, some measure of facility of speech, and a decent level of piety- this is shocking and deplorable. No ministry is worth anything which is not first and last and all the time a ministry beneath the Cross. Let a man reckon the cost ere he closes with the ministry." (James S. Stewart, Heralds of God, New York: Charles Scribner's Sons 1946, pp199-200).

In summation, if God has not called you personally into vocational ministry, do not aspire to it. It will cost you more than you care to give and leave only hurt, broken, and confused people in its wake. If God has called you, humbly accept the call. It will make a difference in your life, in the life of countless individuals, and, most importantly, it will allow the Kingdom of God to move forward.

Key Takeaways:

1) If God has not called you personally into vocational ministry, do not aspire to it. It will cost you more than you care to give and leave only hurt, broken, and confused people in its wake.

2) If God has called you, humbly accept the call. It will make a difference in your life, in the life of countless individuals, and, most importantly, allow the Kingdom of God to move forward.

2

Discovering Leaders You Cannot Afford

In 1984, 1 was called to a new church plant located in Topeka, Kansas. I was not really interested. My family was comfortable, we were in a wonderful church that we loved and had pretty much decided we would stay there for the rest of our active ministry.

For some reason I still do not fully understand, I decided I would at least talk with them. Well, you have a pretty good idea of what happened after that. One interview led to another, followed by a resignation from our comfortable church, and a move to Topeka Kansas.

The church owned five undeveloped acres of land in the Southwest part of the city, and that was it. No parsonage, no office space, and a rented worship space on a retired military Air base. In our first worship service we had sixty-nine in attendance. But they had a dream! And we were captivated by that dream!

Within six months we had raised enough money to begin a

building campaign on the five acres. One year later we moved into a beautiful new worship center. The congregation had grown from that original sixty-nine to over two hundred and I knew I was in trouble.

Yes, the church was growing, we were in a nice new building, and almost everyone was happy, but I was miserable. You see, I knew I was in over my head. Within a space of a little less than two years we had raised more money than I had ever experienced-and spent a lot more; a whole lot more! We were in debt up to our eyeballs. This congregation of two hundred plus people had a mortgage just shy of one million dollars. Remember, this was 1986 when interest rates ranged in the stratosphere of 15% and 16%.

To put this in perspective, our weekly building payment was equal to approximately 51% of our income. Every week we were one week from default. I was not only scared I was petrified. We were where we were because I had allowed us to get there. I had aggressive, vision-oriented leaders, but they did not want to be burdened with worrying about debt payments, infrastructure, or mundane church problems.

When I attempted to speak to these visionaries about our precarious financial situation and lack of sustaining infrastructure, they began to look at me in a different light. Some even began to ask the question, do we have the right pastor? I already knew the answer; they certainly did not have the right pastor! Something had to break, and I was afraid it would be me. I was in the fire and it was scalding hot.

It was at this point God sent me an angel in disguise. He was one of those laymen who was "all in" for the pastor. He never questioned God's call to me as the right pastor for this church. He let me know in no uncertain terms that he would be there for me in good or bad times. He had my back, (and he still does to this day).

In one of our discussions he said, "Well, pastor, we are just going to have to grow ourselves out of this problem." Looking back on that conversation, those words sounded so easy and at the same time so impossible.

I was at capacity. I did not have any more to give. We needed staff, but we were struggling just to keep the doors open. That was when I met Dick. He was a retired farmer and had started coming to our church because of a recent concert he had attended that we had hosted. It was an open seating concert (no ticket sales). Dick and his wife got there late only to find the house was full. I saw them as they turned to leave, and I took them to two seats I knew were still open on the front row. Later, he would describe to me their decision to give our church a try because of that one gesture. He had no idea I was the pastor.

Dick turned out to be another angel God sent my way! After attending for a few weeks, he came to me with an offer. He explained he was a semi-retired farmer and felt that God was directing him to help the Church in some way. After visiting for some time, I asked him if he would be willing to come on staff as an unpaid associate. When he agreed, I felt as if I had won the lottery (never bought a ticket but won the prize). I wrote a job description giving him the responsibility of buildings and grounds. (I should interject here that I had cleared all this with our administrative board ahead of time.)

Dick coming on board gave me the confidence to talk to Carolyn. She was vice president of one of our local banks. She came on staff (unpaid) with the responsibility for finances. After Carolyn I discovered Randy, a retired social worker and counselor who had been attending for some time. He came on board (unpaid) as our "counselor in residence". Randy's job description was to work with all those needing counseling who were filling my calendar daily. Then there was Bruce, a middle-aged, semi-retired, marketing manager who had taken an early buyout. He was fun to be around, never met a stranger, and loved teens. Yep, you got it; he became our (unpaid) youth pastor.

Within the space of six months, I had four staff members. All unpaid, but all so qualified. Dick was a master at handling our buildings and grounds. When we needed a new parking lot, he used his contacts to not only raise the money, but also to do the work. We still use that parking lot today even though it has been resurfaced three times.

It became apparent we needed to refinance our debt. The weekly payments were killing us. Carolyn used her expertise to make this happen. Because of Dick's long time relationship with local bankers, he and Carolyn were able to get us a loan at two-thirds of what we had been paying. We were finally beginning to see some daylight.

Randy, in the meantime, had begun to relieve me of much of the counseling load I had been carrying. As most pastors know, this one area has a tendency to take a whole lot more time than most of us have to give. It was Randy who taught me that if I could not handle most counseling situations in no more than three sessions, I should refer them to a professional who had skills I did not. What a time saver that one piece of advice has been over the years.

Bruce was God's special gift to this pastor and the youth of our church. Within a short few months he had transformed our fledgling youth into a force within our congregation. I wish I could tell you the sense of spiritual fulfillment I would feel when a young person came forward during an altar call. They would no more than get there before just about every young person in our youth group joined them. Many of them would go on to become pastors as well as leaders within our larger community. In fact, many of them are in spiritual leadership positions today, not only in our church, but in many churches around the world. By the way, Bruce is still a member of our church as are his children, grandchildren, and now great-grandchildren. He would eventually yield his position to a younger leader but would tell you without hesitation that the years he served as youth pastor were some of his best.

Dick has since graduated to heaven, as has Randy. Their legacy lives on in the people they touched in those years of serving as volunteer staff. Carolyn accepted a large
promotion at another bank out-of-state after getting us on a firm financial foundation. As I stated earlier, Bruce is still with us, busy loving and engaging with teens. He is one of their loudest cheerleaders.

We continue to use this model after thirty plus years. Today we have twelve staff members, seven paid, five volunteers. All but one has an assigned office, job description, and support staff. Two are serving as part time pastors at one of our new campuses in another part of town. Let me tell you about the staff member who does not have an assigned office, written job description, or support staff. His name is Jeff and he is one of the sharpest businesspeople I have ever met. Twenty years ago, he started a local business from scratch. Today his business spans multiple States employing hundreds of people. Jeff is not only a sharp businessperson but has a spiritual depth that I know pleases God.

It all started with a lunch at a local restaurant. I was quizzing Jeff about his plans for the future. He stunned me with his assertion that he would like to serve on a church staff someday. Now remember this is a person with multiple businesses and hundreds of employees. That day I asked Jeff to join our staff as a lay representative to our group. His job was to bring a layman's perspective to the meetings. It has been three years now and his advice is always quiet but on point. His leadership and love for his church has made us so much better as a staff.

I could tell you stories of Wally, a retired Science teacher who gives as many hours as most of the paid staff. Or Richard or Bill or Jerry or Lois. All giving because they love God and want to serve Him.

Here is the point of this entire chapter. Every church has a Dick or Randy or a Carolyn or Bruce and yes, even perhaps a Jeff. They have a love for the Lord and their church. They have experience, talents, and a desire to serve. They are in every church. Find them and use them. You, your church, and the Kingdom will prosper because of them!

Now for some practical guidelines for placing staff in places of responsibility.

If you are going to invite them onto your team be ready to support them in every way possible. When it comes to finances, make sure you can afford them. Don't make the mistake some do by getting pledges or tapping savings or looking to a select number of individuals to support them. Each one of these paths will lead you to disaster. If the cash flow will not support a staff person, don't make the hire.

Here is a rough guideline you can use when looking at adding additional staff. (I will deal with this in greater depth in another chapter on budgeting) Your staff budget should fall somewhere between 43%-45% of your total budget. If a new hire takes you beyond these borders you are going to have to make some sacrifices somewhere.

When it comes to support, cherish, nurture, defend, and cheer for your staff. The better they do the better you do. Just know whenever you bring a staff member onto the team you are saying to your congregation and existing team members, "This person has gifts and graces that we need and do not currently have."

Never fool yourself. If something goes wrong with a staff member or a responsibility they had, it will eventually land on your desk. Blaming a staff member for a failed project, or not completing an assignment well, will eventually be seen as your failure as well.

It is for this reason that each member added to the team receives the following pastoral admonition: "I will defend you, cheer for you, and support you in every way within my ability. But, if you ever put me in a position where I must choose what is best for you or what is best for the congregation, know I will always choose for the congregation!"

I give this little speech because the first full-time associate I put on the team taught me a valuable lesson. It has been said, "It is good to learn from mistakes, it is even better to learn from other people's mistakes." Here is your chance to learn from one of my early big ones.

His name was John (name changed to protect those not responsible for my lack of wisdom). He came to me as a hurting, humbled, and fallen person. At one time he had been a major player in the evangelistic field of our denomination. Talent, boy, did he have it. He could put a crying baby to sleep with his singing or cause a howling dog to fall quiet. Gifted in so many areas of music and we desperately needed someone with his gifts and talents.

Oh, I did my due diligence alright. I checked out his resume and character references. I talked to people who had worked with him in past days. The composite picture I consistently got back was one of less than stellar recommendations. Two people even called me personally and advised me against the hire. But I really needed someone with his talents, so I simply wrote off those who were advising me against adding him to the staff. In fact, I remember saying to one person who was advocating against him, "That's not the John I know". Boy howdy, did those words come back to bite me.

He came to us as a single man who had been married previously but now divorced. He assured me it was not "his" fault. She had had an affair with another man while he was on the road preaching and singing. (I later learned it was just the opposite.) I ignored all the negative evidence against him because he fit so well in the situation where I needed him to be.

Within two months he introduced me to a lady whom he said he had known for a long time and whose husband had recently died. A few weeks later he advised me they were getting married - the following week. It was at this point I began to think that just maybe I had made a mistake in adding him to our staff. But, once again I looked past the obvious and hoped for the best.

Well, get married they did, and that started another whole series of negative events. I began to hear rumors of spousal abuse and of loud and vulgar arguments, and I knew I was in trouble. Here I had given this individual a second chance at ministry, ignored sound advice and defended him to my ministry board. I called him in a number of times over the following months to see if I could help work out some of his marriage difficulties. He assured me everything was fine, and they were just having minor marriage issues. I, of course, believed him because that is what I wanted to believe. I know at this point you are thinking what an idiot I was. I know that is what you are thinking because that is what I was thinking.

Things rocked along for another few months and I seriously thought everything was getting better. What had in fact happened was they had learned to hide it better. Let me say at this point that I believe God places within us a spirit of discernment at times. When this happens, be advised, listen to it! I did not and it cost me big time!

I had booked a week leadership conference in another state. When I left everything seemed to be in order. No red flags flying. I left feeling pretty good about everything. The day before I returned from the conference one of my board members called to tell me John had resigned effective immediately. He said it was causing quite an upheaval in the church and advised me to return as soon as possible.

Upon returning home I found out John had not only resigned but had moved across town and started a new ministry. All within the one week of my absence. To add a little icing on the cake, he had taken approximately forty of our members with him.

Words literally fail to describe my emotions. Betrayal, yes! Hurt, beyond description! Disappointment, deep and unyielding! Add to this a sense of impending disaster accompanied by a realization of my own culpability.

I learned a valuable lesson that day. Never try to ignore what is in front of you and never try to excuse bad or wrong behavior. It always costs more than you want or are willing to pay.

Whenever I think about this difficult lesson from my past, I am reminded of a story from history.

In 1780 Benedict Arnold was given command of West Point, a strategic American fort on the Hudson River in New York (and future home of the U. S. Military Academy, established in 1802). Arnold contacted Sir Henry Clinton, head of the British Forces and proposed handing over West Point and his men for the sum of one million dollars. To finalize the deal, Arnold met with Major John Andre from the British Army to work out the details. However, the conspiracy was uncovered when Andre was captured with the incriminating papers by the American forces. Arnold, the former American patriot, fled to the British side. George Washington offered to trade Andre for Arnold, but Arnold refused, and Andre was hanged for Arnold's betrayal.

Betrayal is an ugly thing, made only more difficult when perpetrated by those you trust!

Well, we eventually recovered. The ministry John started lasted a total of six months. It imploded when he had an affair with another woman in the church. Within a year almost all forty of those who had gone with him returned. It is good to learn from experience, it is better to learn from other people's experience!

One final thought about staff, paid or unpaid. I strongly recommend weekly staff meetings.

In our early days, I think I intuitively knew about the importance of meeting weekly; I just could not find any advice on how to go about it. Remember, this was before the proliferation of the Internet, where today you can find just about anything, and often things you don't want to find.

I decided to include information on staff meeting agenda in this book because I am convinced you will find it helpful. This was developed by one of our staff pastors to help us be more intentional and productive in our time together.

1) 9:00 a.m. - Prayer
2) 9:05 to 9:30 a.m. - When thinking about what you were a part of this week, what did you do?
3) 9:30 a.m. – Mile Markers
   A) What was supposed to happen this week?
   B) What actually happened?
   C) What can we do better?
4) 9:50 a.m. – Follow up
   A) New Guests
   B) Absentees
   C) Hospital calls
   D) Volunteers
5) 10:00 a.m. – Leadership Development
   10-minute break
6) Calendaring –
   A) This Week
   B) Next Week
   C) Next Month

D) Next Quarter

7) Summary of action Items: Who, What, When

Key Takeaways:

1) When you find yourself over your head or preferably before, get help! Every church has leaders that have a love for the Lord and their church. They have experience! Talents! And a desire to serve. Find them and use them. You, your church and the kingdom will prosper because of them.
2) Listen to your discernment. Never try to ignore what is in front you and never try to excuse bad or wrong behavior. It always costs more than you want or are willing to pay.
3) Communicate and listen! Schedule and run productive weekly staff meetings.

3

The Minister and Time Management

"There is an appointed time for everything. And there is a time for every event under heaven" Ecclesiastes 3:1

†

'Therefore, be careful how you walk, not as unwise men, but as wise, making the most of your time, because the days are evil." Ephesians 5:15-16

Before entering the ministry, I had a small business. I was the only employee. There was no time clock to punch, nor anyone looking over my shoulder to make sure I was investing my time wisely. Accountability came on the last day of every month. My bank account was the auditor. If I had not used my time in a productive fashion, my family and I suffered the consequences.

Whenever you are the only employee, and you own the

business, you have a tyrant for a boss. Forty hours was where you started and seldom if ever finished. You produced or you failed. Time management was not a theory, but a necessity.

Upon entering the ministry, I was—and continue to be—surprised at how some of my colleagues used their time. Let me be clear; I am far from being masterful in the area of time management. It is a daily discipline. It is a discipline I work at and is always before me.

Cardinal J Gibbons said, "There are no office hours for leaders." I have found ministry constrained by hours is nothing short of impossible. After nearly fifty years of pastoral ministry, I have yet to lay my head on the pillow at night feeling I had accomplished everything I should or could have done!

I would advance the thought that one of the major challenges of many ministers lies in the area of time management. There are no time clocks. No one looking over your shoulder to see what you are doing with the one hundred sixty-eight hours a week you have been given. Just you and your sense of what is right and fair to guide you. With that in mind I want to advance some thoughts in this arena.

Time management begins with personal integrity. The story is told of a famous boxer who was training for the biggest fight of his career. In preparation he had laid out a thirteen-mile course which he ran daily.

When asked by a reporter just two days before the event why he did not back off on his running for a bit, his answer was simply, "I am the last person in the world I want to try and fool." Self-honesty is indeed a wonderful thing!

It was Ray Kroc who said, "The quality of a leader is reflected in the standards they set for themselves." We who have the privilege of ministering to God's people would do well to embrace the idea of setting some personal standards for ourselves. This is even truer in the area called time management. The following are some thoughts which might begin to lead us into a life worth inspecting.

Embrace your ministry as a lifestyle and not a job or vocation. Invite your family to participate with you. I say this because it is easy at times to leave your family behind. If your family is constantly feeling as if they are having to fight for your time versus the church, you are in trouble. Take them with you and include them as much as possible.

If you have young children at home, be sure to carve out some time for the one staying at home to have some down time. But a warning here. Be careful to maintain a balance. A good question to ask yourself is this, "If I owned my own business would how I am spending my time be acceptable?"

It is well for each pastor to remember that the church is run primarily by volunteers. In most cases those volunteers will have a responsibility to a corporation or other business for their livelihood. Anything they give to the church will be over and above what they have already given to their employer.

Following are 10 top tips to manage your time better.

#1. Review how you use your time. Keep a diary. Record your entire week and how you invested your time. *Don't* forget to include coffee breaks, telephone calls, hospital visitation, counseling appointments, and sermon preparation. If it is ministry related, include it. At the end of the week, review your diary for time wasters. Things you did but had no lasting value to you, your family, or the church. After you have isolated these, look honestly at them and see which ones really need to be included in your week and which ones should be eliminated. This one thing could save you cherished hours better spent.

#2. Start each day with prayer asking God to help you to use your time in a productive way. After you have prayed, invite the Holy Spirit to reveal to you any place where you are not being a good steward of your time.

#3. Look at your time management through the eyes of an employer, and you are that employer. Would you approve of the way you are prioritizing your time?

#4. Practice Integrity. Be the last person you try to fool. You and only you know the truth about you! Run from excuses.

#5. Be willing to delegate where possible. You can't do it all, nor should you try. Put good people around you whom you can trust. Train them and then turn them loose.

A word about delegation. If you are going to raise up good, talented, and trustworthy people for the work of ministry, you must also delegate authority. Be careful you do not overrule them unless it is absolutely necessary. If they fail, fail with them. Do not use them as a scapegoat to make yourself look good. This is the number one rule of delegation: Just because you have delegated a task does not absolve you of responsibility. If things go wrong, people are still going to hold you accountable. Thus, it behooves you to delegate only to people you trust and don't mind failing with on occasion.

#6. Set realistic expectations. Trying to put too much into a day is a prescription for disaster. Be realistic about what you can reasonably expect to accomplish. A caution: If you fail to set some daily expectations, you will have nothing to measure your day against.

#7. Organize meetings wisely. Do you really need to be there for a meeting to be a success? Don't be afraid to leverage technology. A text instead of a phone call can save you precious time. Sending the agenda out to those involved with the meeting is not only wise, but time saving for all involved. When it comes to e-mails, check them only a few times a day. Any more will distract you and often have you "chasing rabbits." The wise use of technology will help you in numerous ways. Just make sure you are using it, and it is not using you!

#8. Try to limit interruptions. There is nothing more frustrating than to be "on a roll" with a particular project or thought, only to be interrupted by something that could have waited. Turn your phone, e-mail, and other possible distractions off while you are in your "creative mode".

#9. Avoid procrastination. Do that which you really don't want to do first. This also falls into the "priority arena". Learn to push your priorities; don't let them push you. If it must get done, get it done. Organize your day around the highest priority to the least. For me as a pastor, the first thing on my agenda for the week is sermon preparation. I do not allow anything short of an emergency to deter me from the goal of being ready for Sunday. Friday or Saturday night sermon preparation is unwise. You never know what emergency will demand your time. Preparation provides a genuine sense of accomplishment and stress relief.

#10. Spending time in prayer, reflection, and meditation is not a waste of time. In fact, it is a necessary component of becoming the pastor God can and will use. To neglect this part of your personal development is to neglect your own soul nurture.

Time management is not about doing more things. It is about doing the right things at the right time. If you do not control your time, others will control it for you. Embody the idea of living by
priorities and not pressures. You alone are responsible before God on how you use your time.

Our time belongs to God, every moment is His and we are under the most solemn obligation to improve it, to His glory. "Of no talent He has given, will He require a more strict account than our time." (Christ Object Lessons, page 342).

Key Takeaways:

1) Embrace your ministry as a lifestyle and not a job or vocation. Invite your family to participate with you.
2) Time management is not about doing more things. It is about doing the right thing at the right time. If you do not control your time, others will control it for you. Embody the idea of living by priorities and not pressures.

4

Ministers and Money

Let's talk about money. The Bible states: "For the love of money is the root of all sorts of evil, and some by longing for it have wandered away from the faith and pierced themselves with many a pang." 1 Timothy 6:10

Indeed, this thing called money has caused the fall and destruction of far too many pastors.

Because this is a place of many failures, I want to offer some thoughts and guidelines about a minister and money. I am going to break our discussion in half. The first part is "How money is
handled within the church community". The second part is where we will discuss "A pastor's personal finances."

First, it is my firm belief that every church should operate within a budget. It matters not the size of the congregation, nor how much money is raised, a budget can and will become a pastor's best friend.

When I mentioned putting a budget together to a friend in a small congregation, their reply was, "We don't have enough money to budget." It is not the amount you have but knowing what you are going to do with what you have.

The reality is that you never have enough! The budget of my current assignment when I arrived thirty-five years ago was minuscule. Today we wrestle with a million-dollar budget, and still do not have enough.

I am reminded of the story of the Hunt Brothers trying to corner the silver market in the early 1980's. Because of their machinations, the price of silver blossomed from $6.00 an ounce to over $50.00. When asked how much more silver they needed their reply was "Just a little bit more." That seems to be the answer every pastor can mimic when working with the church
budget.

When it comes to church budgeting, allow me to present to you some workable percentages that might help in establishing a budget for your church. These percentages have been hammered out on the anvil of experience and hard knocks. Before we look at that aspect of church budgeting allow me to share with you a story from my early years where I now pastor.

The year was 1985. It was an era of high interest rates and challenging financial times. Our congregation had grown to around one hundred people when we realized we needed to build or stop growing. The space we were renting was quickly becoming inadequate, to say nothing of the headache caused by our parking situation. Fortunately, the church leadership had purchased five acres of land in a rapidly growing part of our city the previous year. We were debt free and felt we really needed to launch a new building program on the beautiful acreage the church owned. But we also knew it was going to take money, a lot of money, and we had little with which to begin the project. We decided on a major fundraising campaign to provide the necessary funds for building.

The congregation was dedicated and excited by the

prospects of "having our own home". After a three-month campaign we had raised almost $400,000. This was nothing short of a miracle. The fervor for building was palatable.

We engaged an architect, who drew up plans for the new building. This took a small, unexpected amount, from our building fund. We were now ready to launch. The day we applied for our building permit, the new church next door to us also launched a building program. There was a two- acre parcel which separated the churches. We had the first option. They decided they wanted that two acres for their building program. We were faced with the problem of either giving up the option to buy the property or to exercise our option. After much prayer and discussion, it was decided we should exercise our option and buy the additional two acres, which we did. This also took a chunk of money from our rapidly depleting building fund.

With building permit in hand, and seven beautiful acres, we were now ready to start construction. Or so we thought. It was not to be. We were instructed that before actual construction could begin, we would need drainage work done and a parking lot installed. Which we did. Our building fund was beginning to show some real strains. To say I was slowly panicking would be a huge understatement. We were down to less than $250,000 and our architect had estimated the building cost at nearly three times that. Our people had just given more than anyone thought possible, and I knew we could not go back and ask for more.

I turned this building program over to God almost daily, yet it seemed that everywhere we turned more money was needed. I started contacting banks to see about a loan to build our much need building. None were interested in taking a huge risk on such a young congregation. We were left with only one option, to sell church bonds to provide the needed capital. We contacted a company that specialized in just such a venture. In a little over four months we sold $500,000 in high interest church bonds. When I speak of high interest I mean in the range of 13-15 percent! We now finally had enough money to begin construction.

About halfway through the actual building program we were once again faced with the prospect of not having enough funds to complete the building. We made some on the fly adjustments and chopped off a part of the proposed project. Within ten months from ground-breaking we were close to completion and almost out of money again. We had made some downsizing modifications to the original plan, but also added in some "things" we felt we simply could not do without. We were over budget by $200,000 and had no idea where to acquire the funds. At the last moment, three laymen from the church and I went to a local banker and borrowed the money personally.

Now for a piece of good news. Within three months of moving into our new building the congregation doubled. Unfortunately, most of them did not give on the same scale as the original one hundred.

Within six months I knew we were in trouble. Our building payments were equal to 51% of our annual income. We laid off staff, I took a major salary reduction and we pinched every penny we could pinch. Each week we were one week away from default on the original church bonds we had sold.

One of my precious church board members tried encouraging me by repeatedly stating, "The only way to get out of this situation is to grow our way out." Eventually that is what we did. God brought some wonderful people to our church who had a shared vision of making a difference in the lives of people and the community. Over a period of five years we were able to once again double our membership.

One of the individuals God brought to us was an executive vice president of a local bank. The family quickly found a church home and we quickly found much needed financial guidance.

This was the person whom I credit with changing the whole way we approached finances. Oh, we had a budget alright, but to be honest, it was really that in name only. We were spending it as fast as it came in, always having to rob Peter to pay Paul.

Within a year our banker had put us on a strict no frills budget. While being compassionate, she also held us accountable. We instituted some percentages which we would budget toward for all payables. I wish I could tell you it was a flawless conversion but that would be untrue. Several people left the church. The common complaint was they felt as if many of their personal and family needs were not being met. It was at this point we began to implement the unpaid lay staff positions spoken about in an earlier chapter.

We have since completed three additional building programs. I would not even begin to think of entering into a building program without a solid budget and knowing how we were going to finance it in advance.

The same holds true for annually putting together a realistic church budget. To attempt guiding a church without a well thought out budget is nothing short of courting disaster. The following is how we do it. It is not a perfect plan, but it works for us. I think it might also work for you with some appropriate tweaking as needed.

We begin the annual budgeting process four months ahead of implementation. Each staff member and department head is asked to submit a request for funding of their ministry for the year. Our finance committee reviews the requests and makes suggestions.

The next process is the actual allocating of dollars. We always use as a base the prior year's income. Our goal is to follow the following guidelines:

Personnel - 43% of proposed budget.
Debt Reduction - 12% of proposed budget

Department Budgets - 15% of proposed budget
Denominational Obligations - 14% of proposed budget
Building Maintenance and Utilities - 4% of proposed budget
General Operations - 7% of proposed budget
Contingency - 5% of proposed budget

These may shift up or down on any given year, but the percentages are what we try to operate within. Now for a couple of closing thoughts about this aspect of church budgeting.

The pastor should never personally handle church money. I speak here from the perspective of the actual, physical money that comes into the church. In addition, the pastor should not be one of the people who can write or sign checks. When it comes to this arena, the best question ever asked about the pastor and money is the one never asked!

Whenever you are budgeting for personnel, never advocate for yourself. Do not make the mistake of trying to budget in a raise for yourself. Let that be handled by your finance chairman or church treasurer. Never talk about your financial situation with other church members. This is nothing short of high church begging.

If you propose a project or new program for the congregation, be ready to offer some financing options. To "propose" without financing options is courting disaster once again.

Now let's spend some time talking about the pastor and her/his personal finances. Once again, personal financial integrity is a character issue. Every pastor should be a generous giver. This starts with the tithe and continues into offerings. If you are not a tither resign immediately. Otherwise you are going to hurt the church and bring dishonor to your calling.

I have known pastors who have said, "I always give my tithe in cash so no one knows what I give." There are two problems with that. First, the tithe is God's - not ours.

Second, it is disingenuous.

If you are truly doing something that edifies the body and honors Christ, why try to hide it? You may think no one knows what you are doing in the giving area, but you are only fooling yourself. Somebody is keeping records someplace, and if you have a giving problem, trust me, people will find out.

When it comes to personal finances, pay your bills on time. I can't emphasize that enough. You represent Christ and the Church. As has been so well stated, "You may be the only Jesus someone sees."

Be careful of credit card debt. The cards are all too easy to obtain, and so difficult to get rid of. If you cannot pay cash, don't buy it with a credit card. I know there are legitimate and necessary times when a person must go "into debt", such as the purchase of a house or needed transportation. Just make sure you can afford the payments.

Some final thoughts. If you are going to challenge your congregation to "sacrificial giving" lead the way as much as possible. Don't ask your people to do what you are not willing to do.

When you go out to eat with others from your congregation, don't be shy about picking up the check. You will find you get a lot more invitations to dine out, and your people will respect you more. Oh yes, be a generous tipper!

This lesson was brought home to me recently when my wife and I were at a local restaurant. It was just the two of us and we were enjoying our time together. The only problem was that the service was really slow and our food seemed to take forever to arrive. When it did finally reach our table, it was not well prepared and on the cool side. Not quite bad enough to send back, but not really appetizing either.

Toward the end of our meal I asked my wife if she thought I should complain to the waitress about our food. Before we were able to make up our mind, the waitress brought our check and laid it down on our table with this remark, "I watch you every Sunday on TV when I have to work and cannot get to my church. Thank you for your ministry to those of us who cannot attend church on Sundays," Whew, was I glad I had not said anything. And yes, I left her a more than generous tip.

One of the hardest lessons I am still trying to learn is that we who serve in a public capacity are on display continually. How we dress, talk, and treat individuals we do not know is so important. We may very well not know someone, but that does not mean they do not know who we are.

Key Takeaways:

1) Every church should operate with a budget. It matters not the size of the congregation, nor how much money is raised, but knowing what you are going to do with what you have.

2) The pastor should never personally handle the church's money. I speak here from the perspective of the active, physical money which comes into the church. In addition the pastor should not be one of the people who can write or sign checks.

3) I would not even think about entering into a building campaign without a solid budget as well as knowing how we are going to finance it in advance.

4) Personal financial integrity is a character issue. Every pastor should be a generous giver. This starts with the tithe and continues into offerings. If you are going to challenge your congregation to sacrificial giving, lead the way as much as possible. Don't ask your people to do what you are not willing to do!

5

A Pastoral Perspective on Caring for People

Hospital Visits

Every pastor has, at one time or another, heard the oft repeated phrase "what a job, you only work one day a week". While those of us in the trenches know this to be untrue, it is correct to assume most of our laymen do not really know how and where we spend our time. That is until they need us, then they rightly assume we will be there for them. And, be there we must.

Every pastor will be faced with making hospital calls, performing funerals and weddings and, at times, offering pastoral counseling. There will be many times in the life of the minister when they will be called upon to provide comfort to a family. Knowing how to provide such comfort will not only honor the God we serve, but also the office we hold. The following are four of the most often repeated needs a congregation experiences where a good pastor cannot only give comfort, but also show those affected that they are being supported.

First, we will look at hospital calls. It is my considered opinion that those confined to a hospital should receive a visit from a pastor daily. How that visit is conducted, and how much time is spent in a hospital room is noteworthy. Remember, with few exceptions, everyone in the hospital is sick or they would not be there. The majority of patients are generally in pain, or at the least uncomfortable. Almost all will appreciate a pastoral call, especially if it is handled correctly. With that in mind here are some general rules and guidelines.

1) Never ask them why they are in the hospital. If they want you to know, they will tell you.

2) Never sit on a patient's hospital bed. There are enough germs floating around in a hospital without you adding to them. Your clothes may be spotless, but they still carry germs that can pose a problem. Also, to sit on a patient's bed is to invade their comfort zone.

3) Never stay for more than five minutes. There will be exceptions to this, but once again remember, they are sick. If you stay longer the patient may feel as if they need to entertain you, which is usually the last thing they want to do.

4) Never interrupt a discussion a patient is having with their doctor or other care giver. This is doubly true if a care giver is providing care to the patient when you arrive. If this occurs simply apologize and come back later.

5) Do wear a clergy badge when appropriate. This helps to identify you to the hospital staff and other care givers.

6) Plan on sharing at least one or two Bible passages with the individual.

7) Always end your visit with prayer.

8) Leave your business card to make it easier for the patient or other family members to contact you if necessary. It will also serve as a reminder to other visitors that you have been there.

9) If a patient shares their medical condition with you, consider it to be privileged communication.

If you follow these simple guidelines, most patients will look forward to your visits. Remember a hospital call is an opportunity to show your care and concern.

Funerals

People will just assume you know what to do when it comes to conducting a funeral. The reality is, if you have never actually preformed a funeral you may find yourself fumbling with exactly what to do and not do. The role of a pastor is crucial during times of loss within the congregation. People are hurting, many times beyond explanation or words. Many times, they will be looking for answers or reasons why their loss has just occurred. Remember your role is more than just offering words of comfort, but to be a listener as well.

Allow me to insert here some thoughts about your pastoral role when a person is dying. If you are indeed invited into this intimate and sacred time, know that the family values you as a representative of God. Never take this for granted but accept it as a privilege. Be careful about falling into the trap of trying to explain why a loved one is dying. Statements like "they are going to a better place", or "God needs them", or "they will be so much better off" should be avoided. Prayer is almost universally appreciated. In these hypersensitive times, allow the Holy Spirit to guide your prayers. Keep in mind there is a ministry of presence, where the best words are never spoken!

If you are present when the individual dies, be sensitive to the situation. If they turn to you for anything it is going to be for prayer. Stay with the family so long as it seems appropriate. Sometimes that will be until the body is removed. Many times, family members will want some personal time with the deceased. This is a good time to make a quiet exit, assuring the family that you will be in contact with them. Never try to do any funeral planning immediately after a person dies. No matter how much you prepare, and think you are ready, you are not. Talking about funeral preparations too soon is not only inappropriate, but insensitive.

Now, let's get back to the funeral preparation. In most situations, a funeral home will contact you about the funeral and the part you will be expected to play. At this juncture the family has met with the funeral director and made some preliminary plans. This will normally include the date, place, and time of the funeral. The call is normally a courtesy call to make sure you are available on the selected date. If the family is requesting the service be held in your local sanctuary, they will need to check for availability.

Now your work begins. First, contact the family to find an appropriate time to meet to plan the service. Here is a general outline to follow when meeting with the family. Assure them that you feel privileged to be a part of the service. Confirm the date, place, and time of the service. Ask if there are any specific scriptures they would like used. Some people will simply draw a blank when asked this question. Many times it is not because they do not know the word of God, but, because they are not exactly sure what scriptures are appropriate. Others will have some already thought out. If they need help offer some of the following options. Psalm 23, Isaiah 57:1-2, Ecclesiastes 3:1-4, John 14:1-6, I Thessalonians 4:14-17, 1 Corinthians 15:50-58, 11 Corinthians 1:3-4, or Philippians 1:21-23.

Ask if they would like the obituary read. If a copy is available, and they would like to have it read in the service, this is a good time to make sure you know how to correctly pronounce each name. If a copy is not available (most funeral homes will post the obituary on their website) make sure to obtain one as soon as possible and go over it thoroughly. If you have a question about a name or other information you will be reading, talk with an appropriate family member. Nothing is more embarrassing to you or a family member whose name is not pronounced correctly.

Ask if anyone would like to give a eulogy. A eulogy is a brief speech memorializing the deceased. This is normally given by a family member or close friend. You can also offer to read letters from family members if they request. Occasionally, as part of a eulogy, the family will wish for a time for others to come forward and share some thoughts. If this is requested, make sure to have a microphone available. It is both agonizing and a little embarrassing for a person to be sharing such intimate moments, and others are unable to hear.

Ask the family if they would like to have some songs or other music included in the service. Once again, they may draw a blank when it comes to thinking about music. Everyone has a preference when it comes to music. Let me be so bold as to offer a few suggestions. *Wind Beneath My Wings*, *You Raise Me Up*, *Time to Say Goodbye*, *It is Well With My Soul*, *In The Garden,* and *Angels*. There is a whole host of others to choose from. When picking music always try and steer them to something appropriate. Also, if the music is a recorded piece, make sure your sound system has the necessary equipment available. If a soloist or group is requested, make sure you can provide whatever they are going to need to accomplish their mission. Provide them a time for practice, and a sound check before the service begins. Making sure you have the proper musicians in place and ready to go will take an enormous amount of stress off you. Each participant should receive a copy of the order of service. Make sure the funeral director has one also.

Some families will want a "slide show" of their loved one's life. They will usually tell you they can put it together. A BIG warning here. Not all systems are compatible. It is beyond awkward for a family to show up thirty minutes before a service and hand you or your sound technician a device not compatible with your system. Be sure you each understand the parameters of your equipment and communicate clearly what those parameters are.

Now you have everything put together for the service. What's next?

On the day of the service arrive at least 15-20 minutes early. This allows you to prepare yourself and to take care of any last-minute situations. If the service is being held at your local church, touch base with everyone who will be participating. Also, make sure you check in with the funeral director. They will be the "go to" person if a situation arises with the family or if anyone has questions you cannot answer.

If possible, secure a room where the family can meet before the service. This allows you to have everyone in one place and they can enter in procession. Normally the funeral director will give some preliminary instructions to the family regarding the service. For example, how they will process in and out, where to sit, and any other pertinent information. When they are finished, you will have an opportunity to pray with the family.

The pastor will lead the casket into the place of meeting. The family will follow behind the casket and be seated. Many times, the congregation will be instructed to stand during the family procession. If this is to happen, it is best to have the funeral director announce it to those in attendance.

There are some minor differences if it is to be a memorial service rather than a funeral. In a memorial service no casket is present. If that is the case, the pastor will simply lead the family in and proceed to the pulpit as they are seated. There are a few different scenarios possible in the service.

At the conclusion of a funeral service some families will request an open casket. Normally the funeral director will instruct the congregation on when they should go forward and view the deceased. It is customary for the pastor to stand at the head of the casket as the people view the deceased for the last time.

After the viewing has been completed and the funeral directors have closed the casket, lead those attending the casket to the hearse. After the casket has been placed into the hearse the

pastor has two options. You can take your personal car or ride with the hearse. If you ride in the hearse, make sure you have a ride back. Most often the driver of the hearse will have to stay until all have departed to take care of the closing of the grave. If you ride with the hearse and have not made provision for a ride back to the church or funeral chapel, you could be at the gravesite much longer than you care to be.

If you drive your own car there are some things you should consider. Try to position your automobile as close to those in the procession as possible. This will do two things for you. First, you will not get delayed in traffic. Second, it will allow you to position your vehicle for easier egress after the service. Otherwise you will be at the mercy of all the individuals parked in front of you.

At the grave site, you will also lead the casket to the place of burial. Be careful not to step on any memorial markers that may be in your path. The pastor will stand at the head of the casket for this brief ceremony. The funeral director will indicate when to begin.

A possible order of service might look like this. Scripture readings (usually two or three). 1 Corinthians 15: 51-52, 54-58, John 14:1-3 and Revelation 14:13 are appropriate scriptures to use. For a believer you could use the following statement, "Forasmuch as the spirit of our departed loved one has returned to God, who gave it, we therefore tenderly commit her(his) body to the grave in sure trust and certain hope of the resurrection of the dead and the life of the world to come, through our Lord Jesus Christ, who shall give us new bodies like unto His own glorious body. Blessed are the dead who die in the Lord."

For a non-believer, the following statement is appropriate: "We have come now to commit the body of our departed friend to its kindred dust. The spirit we leave with God, for we know the merciful Judge of all the earth will do right. Let us who remain, dedicate ourselves anew to live in the fear and love of God, so that we may obtain an abundant entrance into the heavenly kingdom."

For a child, consider the following: "In the sure and certain hope of the resurrection to eternal life through our Lord Jesus Christ, we commit the body of this child to the grave. And as Jesus during His earthly life, took the children into His arms and blessed them, may He receive this dear one unto Himself, for, as He said, "The kingdom of heaven belongs to such as these."

If there are to be Military or Masonic rites, they will commence after your closing prayer.

After all ceremonies have concluded, briefly pay your respects to the family.

Here is a quick outline of components of a funeral I have just written about.

Funeral preparation outline:

1) Meet and get acquainted with the family.

2) Confirm the date, time, and place of the service.

3) Ask if they would like the obituary read.

4) Inquire about any scriptures which should be included in the service.

5) Determine music selections.

6) Ask if there will be any military or other rites included.

7) Ask if there are any special memories they would like you to share.

8) Is there anything they would like to have included that you have not mentioned? (slide show, special speakers, poems, etc.)

9) If there is to be a family meal before or after the service, try and get an approximate number they think might attend. Those preparing the meal need this information.

10) Secure a contact name and phone number for any service clarifications.

11) Pray with the family before they leave.

After you have met with the family and planned your message, put an order of service together.

Suggested order of service:

a) Scripture reading and prayer

b) Music selection

c) Reading of the obituary (if requested)

d) Eulogy (if requested)

e) Open time of sharing (if requested)

f) Music selection

g) Message

h) Closing prayer

If the family requests a simple graveside service, you can easily adapt the above-mentioned format.

Follow up after a funeral with pertinent family members is strongly advised. Although the funeral service itself provides some closure, their new reality is always before them. This is an excellent time to bring the grace of Jesus Christ into their lives in a fresh new way.

A resource we use is published by Stephen Ministries called "Journeying Through Grief". It consists of four short books you can send at various times throughout the year after a loss.

Weddings

As a pastor you will have two primary responsibilities when it comes to weddings. The first involves marriage counseling. When it comes to this aspect of your responsibilities, follow through no matter what. In fact, I might suggest that you not conduct a marriage ceremony without leading the couple through a comprehensive time of preparation. After conducting over three hundred fifty weddings I can tell you the following information is nothing short of mandatory. I have experienced more times than I can remember when couples have decided, in the midst of their counseling, that they were not properly suited for one another! Uncomfortable yes, but better that than a divorce in the future!

For years I struggled through this part of my pastoral responsibility. I say struggled because I always tried to adapt my approach to the couple I was working with. While at times this seemed to work well, it was also inconsistent. I found it was easy to get hung up in one or two issues a couple was struggling with. That was when I discovered a wonderful resource called Prepare/Enrich. This simple tool dramatically changed the way I did marriage counseling. I recommend it wholeheartedly. Caution: There is preparatory work you must do in advance to become certified to use the resource, but I can assure you it is worth your time.

The second part of your responsibility will be to function as the officiant. Be aware that many states have different laws regarding your ability to fill this position. A number will require you to record your Minister's license or Ordination certificate with the county court. That said, some states are quite lax in this requirement. It is wise to check with your state or county officials to determine your responsibility and ability to conduct a wedding. You will have to fill out the wedding certificate, and many states require your records to be on file to do so. While working with couples do not shy away from talking about the importance of Christ in their marriage.

Many times, I have suggested a "no divorce guarantee." It will require one minute a day from both individuals. Here is how it works. Before they part for the day to their individual responsibilities, the man takes his wife's hand and prays for her, asking God to bless, guide, comfort, and keep her in all her activities for the day. When he is finished, the wife then takes the hand of her husband and prays a similar prayer. If they will do this every day of their marriage, they are almost certain to celebrate a silver, golden and perhaps even a diamond anniversary! Christ in a marriage makes all the difference.

The next part you will play is that of officiant. In this capacity you will work with the bride and the groom to put together the ceremony. There are many and varied types of Christian wedding ceremonies. They can range anywhere from the simple to the extravagant.

Most couples will have a general idea of what they would like their ceremony to look like. Your job is to guide them through the process. Remember, in most cases neither of them has walked this road before.

Here is a simple outline you can follow and adapt as needed.

Seating

The family and guests of the bride will be seated on the left side of the aisle, facing the altar, while the family and guests of the groom will be seated on the right.

The groom's grandparents (if available) will be escorted to their seats first. They will normally be seated on the third row right. The bride's grandparents are then seated third row left. The groom's parents are seated next (second row right). The final person to be seated in the wedding party is the bride's mother (second row left).

Prelude music

Ushers seat guests

Candle lighters light candles (if applicable)

Groom's grandparents seated

Bride's grandparents seated

Groom's parents seated

Bride's mother seated

At this point there are many options for how the pastor, groom and respective parties enter. I will note just one option and you can adapt as needed.

Pastor and groom enter

Groom's party enters (best man leads)

Bride's party enters (bride's maids first followed by Maid of Honor)

Ring bearer enters (Stands on right side with groom's party)

Flower girl(s) enters (stands on left side with bride's party)

Bride enters on father's right arm (all stand)

Invite all to be seated when bride and father reach the front of the sanctuary

Begin formal ceremony (once again many options)

"Dearly beloved: We are gathered together here in the sight of God, and in the presence of these witnesses to join together this man and this woman in holy matrimony, which is an honorable estate, instituted of God in the innocence of Eden, and symbolizing the mystical union that exists between Christ and His Church. This holy estate Christ adorned and beautified with His presence and first miracle that He wrought in Cana of Galilee, and Saint Paul commended as being honorable among all men. It is therefore not to be entered into unadvisedly, but reverently, discreetly, and in the fear of God. Into this holy estate these persons present now come to be joined."

"Who presents this woman to be married to this man?" Father answers, ""Her mother and I, or "Her family and I." (Many options once again).

Groom leaves platform and brings bride to the wedding party. Father is seated with mother. Bride is now on the right-hand side of the pastor and groom on left.

The Charge:

(Using bride and groom's name) "I require and charge you both as you stand in the presence of God, to remember that the commitment to marriage is a commitment to permanence. It is the

intent of God that your marriage will be for life, and that only death will separate you. If the vows you exchange today be kept without violation, and if you seek always to know and do the will of God, your lives will be blessed with His presence, and your home will abide in His peace."

Following the charge, the pastor will say to the man:

"(Name), will you have this woman to be your wedded wife, to live together after God's ordinance in the holy estate of matrimony? Will you love, comfort, honor, and keep her, in sickness and health: and forsaking all others, keep yourself only unto her, so long as you both shall live?"

Groom answers in the affirmative.

The pastor then says to the bride:

"(Name), will you have this man to be your wedded husband, to live together after God's ordinance in the holy estate of matrimony? Will you love, comfort, honor, and keep him, in sickness and in health; and forsaking all others, keep yourself only unto him, so long as you both shall live?"

Bride responds in the affirmative.

As an option, the pastor may turn to the parents of the bride and groom and ask:

"Will you, as parents of the bride and groom, and members of God's family, give your blessing to this union?"

All respond together in the affirmative

The couple then turns and face each other holding hands, after bride hands her flowers to her maid of honor.

The pastor will then say, using the groom's name:

"Are you now prepared to exchange your wedding vows?"

The groom answers in the affirmative.

"Please repeat after me. I (groom' s name) take you (bride's name) to be my wedded wife, to have and to hold from this day forward, for better-for worse, for richer- for poorer, in sickness and in health, to love and to cherish, till death do us part, according to God's holy ordinance; and thereto I pledge you my faith."

The minister then turns to the woman and says (using bride's name), "Are you now prepared to exchange your wedding vows?"

The bride answers in the affirmative.

The minister then says to the bride:

"Please repeat after me. I (bride's name) take you (groom's name) to be my wedded husband, to have and to hold from this day forward, for better, for worse, for richer, for poorer, in sickness and in health, to love and to cherish; till death do us part, according to God's holy ordinance, and thereto I pledge you my faith."

Ring ceremony.

Pastor will then ask, "Is there a ring for the bride?" The best man answers in the affirmative and hands the ring to the pastor. The pastor speaks about the sacred symbolism of the ring, and then hands it to the groom to place on the bride's left ring finger. The pastor asks the groom to repeat after him as he places the ring on the bride's finger, "This ring I give you as a token of my love, and as a pledge of my constant fidelity."

The pastor then turns to the maid of honor (who has transferred her and the bride's flowers to a bridesmaid) and asks, "Is there a ring for the groom?" The maid of honor answers in the affirmative and hands the ring to the pastor. The pastor speaks about the sacred symbolism of the ring, and then hands it to the bride who places it on the grooms left ring finger. The pastor asks the bride to repeat after him these words; "This ring I present to you as a token of my love and as a pledge of my constant fidelity."

At this time, you can insert a unity candle ceremony, or a sand ceremony, or a rope ceremony (whatever the couple has decided). If a ceremony is inserted, it is a good idea to place a song or music selection before the ceremony. This gives the bride and groom time to position themselves properly for this portion of the wedding.

After this is completed, the pastor then offers a prayer for the couple and their marriage.

Prayer

Sealing of the vows

"For as much as this man and woman have consented together in holy wedlock, and have witnessed the same before God and this company, and have declared the same by the joining of hands, I pronounce they are husband and wife together, in the name of the Father, and of the Son, and of the Holy Spirit. Those whom God has joined together let no one put asunder."

At this point you can invite the groom to kiss his new bride!

When the kiss is completed have the couple turn (bride

turning to the right to allow her maid of honor to arrange her train) and introduce the couple to the congregation. "It is my privilege to introduce to you for the first time Mr. and Mrs. (Name)."

The couple will begin the processional out, followed by the maid of honor and best man and then bride maids and groomsmen. The flower girl(s) follow the bridesmaids with the ring bearer next. The last person to leave the platform is the Pastor.

The receiving line:

Traditionally the parents of the bride and groom are the first to greet the guests, followed by the newlyweds. If so desired the bride and groom's party can be included, with the bridesmaids first and the groomsmen last.

Some final thoughts:

It is wise to have a trained wedding coordinator to help with all the details of the wedding. Photographs are an important part of helping to preserve the special day. It is a good idea to meet with the photographer before the wedding and set some parameters. If you do not do this, many will take advantage of the situation and become a distraction to the proceedings.

I always recommend that the actual rings not be attached to the ring bearer's pillow. I have had pillows dropped, tossed, kicked, and used as a punching bag. In addition, if you tie the rings on well enough that there is no opportunity for them to fall off; it is going to be difficult for the best man and maid of honor to get them untied without awkwardness.

Pastoral Counseling

Let me begin this part of our discussion about pastoral counseling with some general thoughts and observations.

At one time in my early ministry I found myself doing an inordinate amount of counseling. One day I just stopped and took stock of my situation. I was busy. I was helping people (at least I hoped so), and people seemed to like spending time with me. That was the problem. I was "spending" time but seemed to be receiving little for my investment. When I got absolutely honest with myself, I realized that the majority of people I was seeing on a regular basis in counseling were not really contributing to the growth of the Kingdom, or the forward movement of the church.

It was around this same time I became acquainted with the Pareto principle. Named after the economist Vilfredo Pareto, it specifies that 80% of consequences come from 20% of the causes, asserting an unequal relationship between inputs and outputs. The principle serves as a general reminder that the relationship between inputs and outputs is not balanced. The Pareto Principle is also known as the Pareto Rule or the 80/20 rule.

I accredit the Pareto Principle with revolutionizing how I approach ministry today. John Maxwell, in one of his many leadership books, challenged me to "invert" the Pareto Principle. In other words, instead of spending my time with the 80% who were giving back no more than 20%, what would happen if I began to spend 80% of my time with the 20% who were producing 80% of the positive results in ministry?

Now, I know what some of you are thinking, that lower 20% had some very real needs that should be addressed, and you are right! The real question then was I the right person to be meeting those needs?

I started to think about what could happen if I began to invest 80% of my ministry time in my top 20% of leaders. But that left the question of what to do with all those who had genuine needs whom I would have to forsake if I moved in this direction?

That is where Randy comes into the picture. As you may recall, Randy was a retired mental health counselor looking for a place to perhaps use his gifts at a much less hectic and demanding pace. After a few months of getting acquainted, we came up with this plan. If I were seeing a person for more than three sessions, I would refer them to Randy, who had agreed to work on a sliding income scale. Most would eventually end up paying nothing.

So, what does that say about pastoral counseling? Well quite frankly, a whole lot. In the three sessions I worked with an individual, I could generally pinpoint the core need, at least on a surface level. If I determined that need was in the spiritual arena, I knew I could help them. If their needs fell into areas that I was not trained to handle. I would refer them to Randy.

That one change did so much to improve my ministry assignment. First, it helped to free my calendar, allowing me to begin spending time with my more productive leaders. Second, it kept me from practicing pastoral malpractice. That is, attempting to help people in an area in which I was not trained. Third, it allowed me to help my leaders become more effective in what they were investing their lives towards. It was a win-win for both the church and the pastor. Randy eventually retired from retiring and moved with his wife into a retirement community. Rather than repeat my mistakes from the past, I sought out a skilled, credentialed Christian counselor in our community. I found a gem. Susan is not only gifted in areas I would never be but is very compassionate and Christ centered. She has been an angel in disguise to me as a pastor, and a gift to so many of the people in our church community who have availed themselves of her services.

I would submit to you that there are Randy's and Susan's in just about every community. It may take some time investment and research, but I can assure you it is worth the effort.

Whatever you do, do not fall into the trap of "pastoral malpractice". If you have not received adequate training in counseling, stick to what you do know.

Allow me to share with you how I learned this lesson the hard way. Early on in my present ministry, I had a member by the name of Jim (not his real name). He was one of the young leaders in our church, serving in a number of responsible positions. Jim, like myself was a golfer. Just about every Friday afternoon found us on the golf course. Within a short time, I realized he was not only a quick learner, but beyond sharp intellectually.

Because of my closeness with Jim I was shocked when his wife called me one day out of the blue, to complain about some things Jim was doing that were directly contrary to his normal behavior. She explained that just the day before he had been caught shoplifting from one of our local stores. She also mentioned that he had suddenly started showing signs of extreme agitation with both her and the kids. I was taken off guard because, as I said, we were together almost every week playing golf and I had not noticed any sign of unusual behavior.

I quickly donned my counseling cap and made an appointment with Jim. After three or four sessions he seemed to be getting better. I even assured his wife that I felt like his dysfunctional behavior was the result of his high stress job.

It was just a few weeks later that my phone rang at four o'clock in the morning. We all know when people call at that hour it is seldom good news. On the phone was Jim's wife and she was hysterical. Jim had a gun and was threatening to kill himself. The police were on the scene. She asked me if I would come over and try talk to him. I arrived fifteen minutes later. The police had already subdued him and had called an ambulance. He was placed in the psychiatric ward of one of our local hospitals.

By now I had begun to ask myself some hard questions. What had I missed? Had I triggered something in Jim in one of our sessions? What could I have done differently?

Within a week Jim was diagnosed with a brain tumor. I felt both relief and guilt at the diagnosis. Thirty years later I still ask myself if I could have helped my friend by referring him to someone with professional skills I did not have?

Six months after Jim's diagnosis I stood with his wife and family at his graveside as we said our last goodbyes.

Jim lives on in my heart and in my ministry. He taught me the valuable lesson of not trying to help someone without the proper skills and expertise needed.

Pastoral counseling is a legitimate area of ministry. Our people benefit from it. We just have to make sure we are practicing what we know. Anything contrary is pastoral malpractice.

Key Takeaways:

1) Every pastor will be faced with making hospital calls, performing funerals and weddings and at times offering personal counseling. There will be many times in the life of a minister when they will be called upon to provide comfort to a family. Knowing how to provide such comfort will not only honor the God we serve, but also the office we hold.

2) Practice 5-minute hospital visits. Plan on sharing one or two Bible passages with the individual. Always end your visit with prayer. Leave your business card to make it easier for the patient or other family members to contact you if necessary.

3) When death is eminent or just occurred, prayer is almost universally appreciated. In these hypersensitive times, allow the Holy Spirit to guide your prayers. Keep in mind there is a ministry of presence where the best words are never spoken.

4) When meeting with the family about a funeral, always begin with prayer after greeting the family. Assure them you feel privileged to be a part of the service. Copy and work through a preparation outline and order of service outline.

5) As a pastor you will have two primary responsibilities when it comes to weddings. The first involves marriage counseling and the second is acting as officiant. Copy and work through the outline and sample service order.

6

How to Have an Effective Board Meeting in One Hour or Less

I can still feel the chill of apprehension when, as a new pastor, I realized I had to conduct a monthly board meeting! It was not that I had never been exposed to such, it was just that I had never been responsible to make it happen. Two vastly different things.

I quickly learned that we could, and often did, spend hours of meeting time on ultimately trivial matters. This was not only frustrating to me but also to those who had been elected to guide our Church. I could easily fill reams of paper talking about those frustrations and the conflicts that arose which should never have happened. As an old Dutch proverb says, "We grow *too* soon old and *too* late smart." I hope what I am about to share will help you become a little smarter a little sooner than I did. This is in response to the chaos and lack of productivity which marks many Church board meetings. The really good news is that, as a general rule, you can accomplish all you need to accomplish in an hour or less. As with all situations, however, the content can, and often will, establish the parameters.

Following is an outline I have followed for the conducting of Church Board meetings for the last thirty years. The longest meeting in those thirty years was an hour and a half. That was an outlier. Normally, as I have stated, most averaged about an hour. I have used this outline in a church of sixty with seven board members and in a church of seven hundred with fifteen board members, all in the same location, I will first show you the outline, then return to speak of each item individually.

I. Devotional and prayer time (5-10 minutes)

II. Accepting the previous meetings minutes

III. Information Items (7-10 minutes)

IV. Department Head reports

V. Study Items

VI. Action Items

Now, let's see how this works practically. The first thing you do as the Chairperson (or whatever title you use to describe the one who is responsible for the meeting) is to prepare an agenda using the above described outline. This agenda will be mailed (or e-mailed or messaged or hand delivered) one week prior to the meeting. Teach and instruct each board member that, to be able to discuss something in the board meeting, it must be placed on the agenda one week prior to the meeting. This does a number of things for all involved. Everyone knows in advance what the meeting will entail. Second, because they know in advance what will be discussed, they will have had the opportunity to arrive prepared to address each topic. Third, and best of all---you are not taken off-guard by items and subjects that you are not prepared, or ready, to address. Just doing this one thing will move most meetings along at a much faster pace. As previously noted, the first thing on your agenda will be "Devotional and Prayer Time". The apostle Paul has some great devotional starters. I can suggest a few. 1 Peter 3:1-9 or 1 Peter 5: 1-11. I especially like Paul's letters to Timothy. Chapter 2:1-8, Chapter 3:1-18. Chapter 5:17-25, II Timothy 2:14-26 and, of course, Chapter 4:1-8. These are just a few suggestions. You will, of course, find what fits the time and setting for your board.

The second thing on the agenda is the approval of the last meeting. This is the time to correct or clarify any questions about the prior meeting.

The third thing on your agenda is "Information Items". These are items about upcoming events—many of which have been discussed in previous meetings—and situations happening within the church. It's is also where you can add or update any calendar items. This is, in essence, a glimpse into the flow of ministry within the church

The fourth thing on your agenda is one of the biggest time eaters of the meeting, "Department Head Reports." Here is where you can score some real points with your board and those making the report. Ask them to submit their report one week in advance and include it in the agenda mailing! This includes your treasurer's report. You will be shocked at how quickly your meeting will move along with this one change. When you come to this item, remind everyone they have had the reports for a number of days, and have had ample time to look them over and make critiques. If there is a question or comment about any of the reports, allow time for them to voice such and ask questions.

Caution: This may take some training and patience to change from the previous format of discussing each department report verbally. Just know one or two will resist the change. Don't be dogmatic about it. Eventually they will either see the benefit or be conspicuous in being one of a few making a verbal report. I can assure you most of your members will appreciate the change!

Numbers five and six on your agenda will absolutely transform your board into a much smoother operating group. It is essential for you to implement these changes if you want to transition from long and, at times, acrimonious meetings.

First, a little background. It has been my observation that most elected boards are comprised of two distinctly different personality types. First are the "doers", the "let's get this done" types. Just give them the information and they are ready to make a decision, up or down. The second group is made up of your "contemplators" They want the information, but then they want to think and examine all the details. Each group can easily get on one another's nerves. If you try and pass an item on the agenda to this second group, without giving them time to *think* about it, they will often accuse you of trying to ram something down their throat. This is where the battle could begin and nothing will get accomplished.

Enter number five on your agenda: "Study Items"

Study items are things you are looking at and eventually voting on. In this phase you do not vote but propose and give information. For instance, let's say it is nearing the time for the church to purchase a new van. Rather than just presenting the idea and throwing it out for all to give their opinion, and they all will have one, present the idea. Give the merits of why this is the time to begin to move towards buying a new van. Listen to those who have the loudest voices about the future purchase. Appoint some of them to a committee to study the idea and bring a report back to the next board meeting, where it will once again be submitted as a Study Item.

If there is merit in purchasing a new van, ask the committee to go back and research all the pertinent information regarding the van. For example, type, model, color, financing, and to bring a report back to the next board meeting where it will continue to be a Study Item. During this time there will be plenty of interaction and opinions concerning a van purchase. After all the information is gathered, and all questions answered, it will then be moved to an "Action Item".

Which brings us to number six on your agenda "Action Items".

Action items are items which have gone through the study item process and are now ready to be voted upon. Everyone has had at least a couple of months to think, interact, research, and give opinions. NOW you call for the vote.

I have used this method to hire additional staff, build new buildings for our current location, pass budgets with little or no opposition and yes even the buying of new vans. Seldom when it gets to the Action Item, is much time taken up in discussion. This has already occurred in the "study mode". I have seen million-dollar budgets, and large building programs approved in a matter of minutes using this tool, and you will also.

Something You Should Consider:

The process I discussed above works! A caveat needs to be expressed at this point. Do not attempt to implement this in one month, or even a number of months. This is especially true if you are new to your assignment. Introduce it slowly. Talk about its merits. Maybe even introduce parts of it at a time, with the hope of having it totally in place within a year to eighteen months. Keep in mind the personality types you have on your board. Knowing your board will save you from a lot of stress and turmoil.

If you are so fortunate as to be starting a new church from the ground up, you will find this process much easier to implement. Don't hesitate. Start your first meeting with the process outlined.

Key Takeaways:

1) Board meetings can quickly become bored meetings. Things will move along faster and keep everyone engaged by being agenda driven.

2) Go slow in implementing change.

7

Building Campaigns

We built our first building in 1986. We have added to that first building three times. Those times of building were some of the most challenging and taxing of my ministry. Today, if you were to suggest to me another building campaign, I think I would run and hide!

That said, building campaigns are a necessary part of a growing and expanding church.

I want to share some insights I gained from those four building experiences.

Before I get into the specifics, let me make some overall observations. First, if a building campaign is in your future, decide before you build that you are committed to building and staying. I cannot begin to tell you how many pastors do just the opposite. It seems, too often; when a building campaign is completed, God just happens to call the pastor to another assignment. Now please understand, I don't blame them for moving but it is just wrong! Building-and-running does a tremendous disservice to the church and to the community.

Also, the pastor who replaces you must pick up the pieces and buy into a vision God gave the previous pastor.

Buildings cost money; a lot of money. The pastor is responsible to insure the money is raised. Have a plan.

We will talk more about this later.

Be ready to commit not only your time, gifts, and effort to the campaign, but also your own personal finances. You should always lead where you are asking the people following you to go. One thing I can assure you, if you do not do this one thing the campaign will fail.

Have a vision for what you are proposing. The prophet Habakkuk provides some guidelines for a vision: "I will stand on my guard post and station myself on the rampart; And I will keep watch to see what He will speak to me, and how I may reply when I am reproved. Then the Lord answered me and said, record the vision and inscribe it on tablets, that the one who reads it may run. For the vision is yet for the appointed time; it hastens toward the goal, and it will not fail. Though it tarries, wait for it; For it will certainly come, it will not delay."

Note a few things about the above passage: First, it reminds those of us charged with the ministry of shepherding that we are the guards. We must never endanger the people we are called to shepherd. Next, we are to stand above the normal and mundane and position ourselves to see what others cannot. We are to be listeners of the Divine. If there is anything in our own personal life that would hinder us from hearing God's voice, it needs to be addressed and taken care of. Then and only then will God begin to impart a vision to the shepherd. When it comes to things of such importance and significant impact as a vision for the future don't be unduly influenced by the people around you.

In another church, some time back, I had one of our lay leaders come to me and say, in regard to a needed building expansion, "If you don't do this now it will never get done." I did it, not because of a vision God had given to me, but because of pressure from people. We built the building alright, but it cost so much more than any of us had anticipated. I will not go into details here, but suffice it to say, that after the building was finally completed, I left the pastoral ministry for a number of years. Little did I know I had four building programs in my future as a pastor. Be guided by God's vision, not by man's wants and perceived needs. Have a plan for the vision you are proposing. A vision without a plan is only a dream! Talk to others who have gone through where you are going. Listen to what they have to say. Listening does not mean you are going to adopt everything they impart, but it will help to give perspective.

Do your research! Know your church history. Ask yourself the hard questions: Why am I doing this? Has God spoken to me, or am I simply responding to a perceived need? Am I willing to "stay and pay"? Can I commit my family and our personal finances to the project?

Here are a few things you will need to have in place as you proceed. After you have ascertained that God is directing (this is often your first big faith move), you will need to research your spiritual and financial position. Some questions like: Is there unity in the church? Are there presently any pressing problems which might hinder or distract? Are you, as the shepherd, in a place where you can give overall direction to the program? Is there potential financial backing for the project? Is the timing right?

If all your questions are answered in a faith-based, fact-centered way, then you are ready for the next step.

Begin to talk your dream with the key leaders of your church. Listen to them carefully. If they are not in agreement with the vision, it is going to be extremely hard to move forward. If they are captivated by your thoughts and plans, they will become your initial team of visionaries. You will need them as you proceed.

Usually the first question that will arise is, "Can we afford this?" That is a fair question you should be ready to discuss. What they will really be asking is where is the money coming from?

Let me share some practical thoughts about building expansion financing. First, rule out long term financing. In other words, don't borrow to build! If you go in that direction it will eventually cause you long term difficulty. You will be financing your future, closing the door for staff enhancement; other church building improvements will not happen as quickly as necessary and you will be robbing people of direct ownership. Often the building will need significant improvements before the mortgage is paid off. Also, buyer's remorse can set in. (Remember that new car which just begged to be bought but lost its luster long before the payments were completed).

There are some merits to short term borrowing. When I speak of short term, I am speaking in the range of six months to a year. A better solution is to have enough money banked to begin your program. You will need to have in the area of five to ten percent of your total program to get started.

What do you do if you do not have that kind of money available? Consider a "Capital Campaign" to finance your entire budget. In fact, even if you do have enough money to get started, at some point you are going to need more. The reality is you will spend between ten and 15 % of your entire program budget before you ever break ground!

A capital campaign is an intense effort on the part of a nonprofit organization, to raise significant dollars in a specified period of time. It is a targeted fundraising effort designed to provide the necessary funds for any specific project. The big question is where to begin? There are two ways to accomplish your capital campaign goal. I have experienced both.

Before we go into greater detail, let me give you some

general guidelines. The best scenario is to attempt to receive pledges over three years. Any longer and you will experience diminishing return. It is best to get your more financially secure individuals on board before you start. This will give you a head start when you enter into the actual fundraising stage. Make sure your plan is ready for launch. Timing is everything.

Now back to the "how."

The first way is to do it yourself. What I mean is do all the research necessary for a successful capital stewardship campaign. This is a major task, but not impossible. You will need to do your homework and be prepared to invest a good bit of your time in the process. The big benefit is the amount of money you can potentially save. The downside is you will not raise as much money as you could have.

I will explain that later.

The second way is to align yourself with a professional fundraising company. They provide wonderful expertise. If you enter into a contract with them, they will provide everything you will need for a successful campaign. With their expertise and insight, they can help lead you through the campaign, from a feasibility study to the end of the campaign as well as to provide follow up. It will cost you. The cost varies but will fall somewhere between eight and 15% of the total project. The greater the project the smaller the percentage.

As related at the beginning, I have done both. I suggest you go with a professional campaign company. Yes, it costs a lot of money, but it will pay dividends in the end. Think about it this way. If you had an infected tooth you could possibly take care of it yourself. But wisdom would seem to indicate a dentist would be the better option. They have the proper tools and experience to provide you with some relief. The same holds true when it comes to any situation in which you find yourself without the tools or experience. If you do not know what you are doing, defer to the experts!

A few years ago, after going through three building campaigns, we found ourselves in need to expand once again. We had all the materials from the previous capital campaigns. I felt like we could do this ourselves. I selected one of the sharpest laymen in the congregation. He was a gifted speaker and organizer, and more than anxious to lead our campaign. He took all the information from our past campaigns and forged them into a program of his own. He made charismatic presentations to our people. He got our strongest financial people to buy in. The advertising material and campaign brochures he designed were beyond excellent. We did everything in this campaign that we seemed to have done in the prior ones. When the money and three-year pledges were tabulated, we had fallen 35% short of our goal!

Our people were shocked, and I was dismayed. It seemed as if we had done everything right. But we had failed.

Let me interject, in these kinds of situations, you only get "one bite at the apple". We could not go back to our people and ask for more money. Most felt they had given all they could. To add to the difficulty, we had pledged to our congregation we would not borrow money for the project. In one sense, we had a lot of money we could do nothing with.

So, what went wrong? To this day I'm not sure I can give you a definitive answer. But, one glaring statistic stands out; we had not used a professional organization to help us.

Please understand I am not a spokesperson for any Capitol Campaign organization. But I am, now and forever, convinced that professionals are called such for a reason! A fair question is how do you pay for a capital campaign consultant? In our prior three campaigns we had a "first fruits offering". This was really the culmination of the actual work of the campaign and the beginning of collecting the money.

In each of those first three "first fruits" offerings we

received enough money to pay our consultant, and to begin our design work. We were also able to pay back any short- term loans we had incurred to begin the campaign.

One final observation. Attempting to pay cash for a building of any substance is difficult to impossible. You will ultimately stymie the forward progress of the church and discourage your people. It sounds wonderful to say that you are paying as you go, but seldom is the approach successful. I know I have just annoyed some individuals, but beware. Your good, vision-oriented people will not stick with you as you attempt a pay-as-you-go program. Please understand, I am talking about major building programs, not small repair or upkeep situations.

Key Takeaways:

1) New buildings costs money; often lots of money. Know what your financial situation is and plan within your ability to pay for the program.

2) Using a professional to help you raise funds will cost you short term, but will quite often, pay long term benefits.

8

Understanding the Power Structure in the Local Church

"Leadership is the capacity and will to rally men and women to a common purpose and the character which inspires confidence." *Bernard Montgomery, British Field Marshall*

A number of years ago, and almost in another lifetime, I was called to be the senior pastor of a new church plant. The church had started with a few laymen who wanted to establish a new work in a new and growing part of the city. The leadership was excited, forward looking, and positive about what God could do through them in establishing this new work.

At the time of my arrival the new congregation had been meeting for months without permanent pastoral leadership. During this time, they had seen many new families join them, and the excitement level was quite high. There was a sense of God's anointing and blessing on the church.

Everything went pretty well for the first six months or so. There came a day when I felt it was important to begin adding more spiritual depth to our group. I began to implement some changes I thought would help us achieve this goal. That was what I came to call the beginning of "sorrows."

I had spoken to our church board about the implementation of said changes, and they were on board. The problem was I had not "cleared" the idea with the self-appointed leadership team; and I was in trouble!

It was at a breakfast meeting a few days later that I was told the changes were "half baked" and needed to be looked at more closely. The suggestion was made that the proposals be put on hold for the time being and that I should worry more about other priorities.

It was at this point I wished someone had reminded me that not all leaders of a local church are elected, or sit in any elected decision-making position, yet wield vast power. In fact, in many situations, these unelected leaders are often much more influential than those elected to lead.

The hard reality is that people follow leaders. Leaders are most often chosen because of their influence. In fact, I believe leadership is indeed influence. Influence is the power to have an important effect on someone or something. Sometimes people can and will use their influence to benefit themselves rather than the intended situation. That being so, the wise leader will move slowly when making changes to those currently leading, whether elected or otherwise.

The trap I had walked into as the new pastor was that there had already been established a clear group of leaders, and few of those were elected. Looking back, I so wished I would have recognized and accepted this fact and learned to work within the existing power structure. I would have avoided some very real bumps, bruises, and contusions. In addition to this, I believe the church would have moved forward much quicker.

A thought: If you are beginning a new assignment don't attempt to destroy, remove or alter the existing leadership you inherit for at least a few years. Learn to work with what you have, not what you want. Eventually, if indeed your ideas are better and new leadership is required, go about the change slowly and with much prayer and God-sought wisdom. Any other direction will quite often fail for lack of acceptance by those who have the most influence, and you will find yourself and your ministry floundering. One of the great values you bring to the table is mainly what you can get done through others. Once again, work with what you have, not what you want.

Perhaps the following six things will help you as you navigate leader-shift.

#1. Approach every change with a positive attitude. This does not mean you necessarily like the change, but if it is inevitable, accept it and adapt. Never allow your feelings to get in the way of the necessity of a situation. Happiness and a positive attitude are not synonymous and should not be aligned as such. A positive attitude is finding and exploiting the good in a given situation while marginalizing the negative.

#2. Be futuristic in your thinking. Don't allow yourself to be held to just what you know and have experienced. A wise man once said, “Dream as if you were going to live forever, live as if you were going to die tomorrow.”

#3. Be open and flexible to new ideas and possibilities. Refuse to be intimated by something you have never heard about or tried. The frontier of discovery is waiting to be conquered.

#4. Think globally. Strive to see the big picture. Think of the difference a caterpillar sees as he traverses his universe and what the butterfly sees while looking upon the same universe.

Ask God to help you grow wings and fly.

#5. Communicate clearly. People do not fear change nearly as much as they fear the process of change. Communicate with empathy, compassion, and wisdom. Give your followers a chance to metabolize the future you are presenting. Don't be in a rush. You have probably lived with the idea for some time, give those you are leading time to catch up with you.

#6. Don't allow opposition to a good idea derail you. If it is a good idea, expound on its virtues while listening to your opposition. Many great ideas have been born out of the clarifying thoughts from those who are opposed. As stated in #3, be flexible and adaptable.

Learning to work within the existing leadership structure is not only wise, but necessary, if you are going to have a positive impact on those you are called to lead. Never forget, the one who gives you the most push back could actually be your greatest teacher. If you manage to navigate the critical people you are leading, you will find your own leadership changing and developing in a more positive way.

Finally, when working within the existing leadership structure, always look for the win. Stephen Covey calls this the "win/win principle.” If a person or leader thinks they are going to lose, they will fight all the harder for their position. The wise leader will look for the balance found between winning and losing.

Key Takeaways:

1) Not all leaders are elected or appointed.

2) Influence is leadership.

3) Remember, it is not about you, but about God and His Kingdom

ABOUT the AUTHOR

Larry D Holmes has been the pastor of Wanamaker Woods Church of the Nazarene in Topeka, Kansas for the past thirty-five years. He began his assignment in 1985 when the church was a new home mission church plant. His first Sunday service there were sixty-nine people present.

During his tenure as pastor, the church has received over 1,000 new members. Out of his ministry has flowed numerous pastors, missionaries, and church leaders.

Dr. Holmes lives in Topeka with Jolene, his wife of fifty-five years. They have two daughters, five granddaughters, two sons-in-law and one grandson-in-law.

The Holmes' have made their Sunday dinners a family tradition. With three generations around the table, the subjects debated, discussed, and shared are lively and wide-ranging. It is here that Pastor often finds inspiration for the topic of a new book.

With the number of freshly graduated ministers Dr. Holmes has taken under his wing, it is no surprise that he should write *Everything They Didn't Teach You in Seminary*. So willingly sharing his knowledge and years of practical experience is what has made him a most beloved figure in the Nazarene church community.

OTHER BOOKS
BY PASTOR HOLMES

PRINT

Faith is for the Living

Available through Amazon
And as an ebook through most every ebook publisher,
including Amazon and Barnes & Nobles

E-BOOKS

Who is King?
Fearless Living
Life's Delicatessens
I Can Because I'm Blessed

Available through most every ebook publisher worldwide,
including Amazon, Barnes & Nobles, Kobo, and Apple.

†

www.ingramcontent.com/pod-product-compliance
Lightning Source LLC
LaVergne TN
LVHW091120150826
845673LV00002B/909